"To those who shared their knowledge, experiences, and wisdom with me, my sincere gratitude for enriching this book with your collaboration."

Bruno Baldaccim

This Book Belongs to:

_____

ALL RIGHTS RESERVED©
2024

No part of this publication may be reproduced, distributed, or transmitted in any form or by any means, including photocopying, recording, or other electronic or mechanical methods, without the prior written permission of the publisher, except for brief quotations incorporated in critical reviews and other specific noncommercial uses. Any unauthorized replica of this work is prohibited.

W.T.C.P©
Weird Talking Crow Publications

Test Color Page

www.ingramcontent.com/pod-product-compliance
Lightning Source LLC
Chambersburg PA
CBHW062120220526
45471CB00010B/3806